# Report and Term Paper Writing

## BY
## REBECCA DYE, Ph.D., and KIM DICKHUT

COPYRIGHT © 2002 Mark Twain Media, Inc.

ISBN 1-58037-203-1

Printing No. CD-1549

Mark Twain Media, Inc., Publishers
Distributed by Carson-Dellosa Publishing Company, Inc.

# Table of Contents

# Introduction to Teachers

We hope you will find this book a common-sense approach to helping students learn how to conduct and write research appropriate for short reports as well as more lengthy term papers. It is not intended to replace your current instruction on library skills or organizing information. It is intended to supplement and extend what you are currently doing. Hopefully, it will aid in moving your students toward better organization and more critical thinking, decision-making, independence, and creativity in their presentation of research.

We have compared the process of writing reports and term papers to taking trips, with reports being fairly short trips requiring less baggage, fewer changes of clothes, and a more focused itinerary. Because a term paper is a more complicated assignment requiring more research skill, resources, organization, and presentational form, we compared it to a longer trip with more carefully identified baggage, use of a passport (library card), and an expanded itinerary. Students are provided with a variety of responses/decisions, examples of student work needing their input, and writing exercises to sharpen their own skills.

# Introduction to Students

Being assigned a report or a term paper involves asking the right questions and finding the answers to those questions. Interestingly enough, those questions are almost exactly the same questions you would ask if you suddenly learned that you were going to be leaving on a trip. Chances are you would ask some, if not all, of these questions! *Where will I be going? How will I be traveling? How long will I be staying? What kinds of things will I be doing while I am there? What will I need to take with me?*

This book is designed to help you learn how to ask and answer those questions, as well as how to properly label your luggage (tell where you found your information), take clear pictures, buy the best souvenirs (take good notes), and tell everyone what you saw and did while you were there. In other words, you will be able to write a report that is interesting and makes sense to your audience. This book is not meant to replace your tour guide (your teacher), and it is not meant to replace your ticket agent (your librarian or resource center director). You NEVER want to take off without them! But with their help and the suggestions from this book, we think you are going to have a wonderful trip!

Name:_____ Date: _____

# Chapter One: *Where Are We Going?*

## Destinations, Topics, and Titles

So your teacher has given you the assignment of writing a report or a term (research) paper. In many ways, being assigned a report—but not knowing what the report is to be about— is like being told that you are going on a trip but not being told *where* you are going, *when* you are going, *how* you are going, or *how long* you will be staying.

If you were told you are going to be taking a trip, what would be the first thing you would ask? Why would you want to know that?

_____

_____

_____

_____

Your teacher will be giving you useful details about that report or term (research) paper. Among the most important details you will want and need to know are these.

## 1. TOPIC

Will the teacher give you a topic, or will you need to decide on your own?

Sometimes, the teacher will give each person in the class the same general topic and will want each person to find and report on the same basic information. That is a good way for students to begin to learn about topics on their own.

At other times, the teacher will give each person in the class the same general topic and will expect each person to choose something about that topic that really interests him or her. The purpose of this assignment then becomes not only a way for each student to do research, but also a way for each student to look for information that really interests him or her.

Doing this kind of report is much like being told that you and your family are going on a trip to New York, Chicago, Los Angeles, or New Orleans. Unless you will be staying in one of these cities for years and years, you will probably not get to see or do everything that city offers.

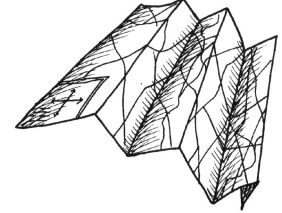

Name: _____ Date: _____

# Chapter One: *Where Are We Going?*

Think about the people in your family and what each person would want to do. Some people can't wait to go to the city because they want to spend their time visiting museums. Some people like to spend all their time at certain historic sites, theme parks, or tourist attractions. Some enjoy spending all their time shopping, or eating, or going to see plays. What you plan to do would make a big difference in what you want and need to take along!

It is the same idea when you are doing research for a report or term paper. If you were to do a report on New York City, you would need to know if you were supposed to talk about all of New York City, or if you were to choose only one thing about New York City and write about that.

So let's give this a try! Let's pretend that you have been asked to write about the whole city of Chicago, Illinois. What kinds of things do you suppose you would need to include in your report?

_____

_____

_____

_____

Share your ideas with at least two other people in a small group, or your teacher may want to have the whole class give responses. How many on your list were the same things someone else listed? What did each of you list?

Now, let's pretend you are supposed to write a report on Chicago, Illinois, but this time you are supposed to write about just one aspect—one thing—about Chicago that really interests **you**. Write one or two things you would like to know or explore about Chicago.

_____

_____

_____

_____

Share your ideas with at least two other people in a small group, or your teacher may want to list everyone's answers on the board. How many of these topics are the same? Which kind of report would **you** *rather* write?

4

Name:_____ Date: _____

# Chapter One: *Where Are We Going?*

### 2. PURPOSE

While the topic is very important, it is even more important to be sure that you understand why you are doing this assignment. The reason **why** is not just because your teacher says you need to do this! Your teacher asks you to do certain things in a certain way so you can learn both *facts* **and** *skills*. Understanding the *purpose* of this assignment will help you learn more about the process and will help to improve the project you produce—the written report or research paper. Are you to answer specific questions? Are you to find specific facts? Are you being asked to convince your reader about something? Are you being asked to compare and/or contrast two different things? Are you supposed to analyze a subject, and then simply state your findings? In addition to learning much about your topic, what kinds of things will you be learning to do? Will you be learning how to use sources in your school library/media center? Will you be demonstrating that you understand how to organize information?

Once you know and understand the purpose of your report or term (research) paper, and once you know your topic, you will also need to know a few other things, such as:

A. **The required length of the report ...** Knowing the required length of your report is important because it will tell you if your teacher expects you to give general information or very specific information. For example, if your report is to be no longer than three pages, and you are to write about New York City, then you should know that you are looking for some fairly specific details.

B. **The number of sources required for your report ...** A source of information could be a book, a magazine, an encyclopedia, a video, or even a brochure. But it could also be an interview with a person, a map, a letter, an e-mail, or even information from a website. Does your teacher want you to use *all* or only *some* of these sources? Will you be able to find and use all your necessary sources at school, or will you need to do some of your work at home or at your public library?

C. **What the finished report will look like ...** When you have finished finding your information, does your teacher want you to hand-write it, or will you need to use a computer and type it? Are you to include pictures, diagrams, or maps? Are you supposed to tape record or video record your report? Are the pages supposed to be put into a binder or a cover of some kind? Will you need to be ready to share your report with the class with some kind of class presentation, or will your report be on display for others to see?

D. **When the finished report must be complete ...** Knowing exactly when your report is due will help you plan the best way to use your work time.

Name: _____ Date: _____

## Chapter One: *Where Are We Going?*

Now let's pretend that when your teacher gave you the assignment about Chicago, you were given these details.

1. Your report is to discover information about a famous person who was born in Chicago **OR** a person who became famous while living and working in Chicago. (Your teacher has provided a list from which each student will choose a different famous person.)

2. You must prepare a five-page report that you type, using a computer or word processor. In addition to the five pages of your report, you are to include at least two exhibits in an appendix section, and you are to provide a "Works Cited" page. This means that your entire report will need to be at least eight pages long.

3. You must use at least five different sources in your report. These may include such sources as books, magazines, brochures, an interview, e-mail, or a map or atlas.

4. You will have two weeks to work on this project. You will have one hour each day to go to your school's library/media center for doing research and for typing your report on a computer or word processor. (You may have more time during the day if you've completed other work and are permitted to go to the library/media center.)

5. You will have today's class time as a "plan your work" day. Planning is very important! If you don't know what information you are looking for, you will end up wasting your time and becoming very frustrated in the library/media center. So, let's pretend that the famous person who is the subject of your report is Jane Addams. Do you know anything about this person other than the fact that she has something to do with Chicago? Jot down what you know or think you know about her.

_____

_____

_____

_____

Now, let's pretend that you don't have a CLUE about why she is famous. (Are we still pretending?) Start your *pretend* report by jotting down six to ten questions you would want to know about this lady.

1. _____    2. _____

3. _____    4. _____

5. _____    6. _____

7. _____    8. _____

9. _____   10. _____

     

Name:_____ Date: _____

# Chapter One: *Where Are We Going?*

Good job! Now, since others in your class have just completed the same task, compare your questions with at least two other classmates and see how many of the same questions you share. Are there any questions that only you asked? Did someone else come up with a question that is more interesting than one you asked?

Now, looking at your questions, try to think of what kinds of sources would be the best places to find the answer or answers to those questions. Remember, you are supposed to use five different kinds of resources. Which kind of resource would be best for which question?

1. _____    2. _____

3. _____    4. _____

5. _____    6. _____

7. _____    8. _____

9. _____    10. _____

Now, look at your questions again. Which questions would you need (or want) to answer first? Second? Put them in the order they should be answered.

1. _____    2. _____

3. _____    4. _____

5. _____    6. _____

7. _____    8. _____

9. _____    10. _____

Great! Since we are still just pretending, let's think about the whole issue of planning your work. How long does your class really meet every day? (This is important since your

 teacher said you would be having class time to work on this project.) Now be VERY honest! If you selected the questions about Jane Addams that you planned to answer in your report *before* you went to the library or media center, do you think you could find the answer to at least one question each day?

_____

_____

Name: _____ Date: _____

# Chapter One: *Where Are We Going?*

Can you think of one or two reasons why your task would be easier if you thought about your focus questions BEFORE you went to the library/media center? List the reasons here.

_____

_____

_____

_____

Do you think you could write out the answer in a way that would be nearly ready to include in your final copy?

_____

Why might that be a good idea? _____

_____

How many students are in your class, how many computers are available for your class to use, and how much time do you usually need to type one page?

_____

_____

_____

Considering your ability to type and the computers available to use, would it be more efficient for YOU to try to answer and type one question a day (always saving your work), or would it be better to answer all the questions, then type your entire paper?

_____

_____

_____

What types of "exhibits" (pictures, charts, maps, brochures, etc.) might you want to include in your report about Jane Addams? Remember, you are to include two of these exhibits in your project. What types of exhibits would work with the questions you have decided to ask and answer in your report?

_____

_____

_____

_____

Name:_____ Date: _____

# Chapter One: *Where Are We Going?*

Last, but not least, you will need to decide on a title for your report. While you might be tempted to simply use *Jane Addams*, it wouldn't really be true because you couldn't possibly say all there is to say about her in only five pages. Look at your questions again. Do any of your questions suggest a particular aspect of her life? Sometimes it is easier to decide on a title that really says what your report tries to say AFTER you have completed your research. Since you haven't done your research yet, see if you can create a few interesting titles based only on the questions you would want to answer. Your titles can be statements or even very short questions—just not the questions you will answer in your report! For example, if you had written a report on me (and I can't imagine why you would ever want to!), you might find any of these titles appropriate:

**Jane Addams**

*Dr. Dye—A Teacher's Teacher*
*Dr. Dye—Better Living Through Language Arts!*
*Books Are Her Life—Why Dr. Dye Writes Them*

Now looking at the questions you would want answered about Jane Addams, generate a few possible titles.

1. _____  2. _____

3. _____  4. _____

5. _____  6. _____

Share and compare your titles with two or three students in your class, or your teacher may want to list all titles on the board. Which one do you like best and why?

_____

_____

_____

_____

_____

*Congratulations!* You have just learned one of the MOST valuable lessons in doing research for a short report or a longer term paper. Being organized (knowing your task and doing some *smart* planning that includes generating questions and estimating the work time needed) allows you to enjoy your work and produce a better finished product in less time. (Hey, is this great or what!)

Name: _____ Date: _____

# Chapter Two: *Planning Your Stay*

## Organizing and Outlining Your Work

When we think about taking a trip, we naturally think about all the things we want to do after we arrive. For example, think about the kinds of things you would want to do if you were going camping in a tent for five days at a state park. On your first day, you will be arriving and setting up your campsite. On the fifth day, you will be taking down your tent and preparing to leave. What do you think you might do on such a camping trip?

On your own, list some activities.

### My List

1. _____     2. _____
3. _____     4. _____
5. _____     6. _____
7. _____     8. _____
9. _____     10. _____

Now that you've made your list, compare it with at least one other classmate. How different is his or her list compared with yours? With the help of a partner, produce a revised list including things that were on both lists. If you had different activities listed, you will need to discuss and decide which activities will be included because your revised list may name only eight different activities. (Some activities may be repeated, so mark things you would probably do more than once with an "R" for "repeat.")

### Revised List

1. _____     2. _____
3. _____     4. _____
5. _____     6. _____
7. _____     8. _____

Great! This sounds like it's going to be a lot of fun!

Name:_____ Date: _____

# Chapter Two: *Planning Your Stay*

Take your revised list and, with the help of your partner, think about the kinds of tools, clothes, equipment, or *stuff* your activities will require. Some of these things you would need to provide. Mark the things you will need to bring with an "M" for "me" and things the park would provide with a "P."

## Revised List

**Activity #1** _____

Stuff needed:  a. _____

b. _____

c. _____

**Activity #2** _____

Stuff needed:  a. _____

b. _____

c. _____

**Activity #3** _____

Stuff needed:  a. _____

b. _____

c. _____

**Activity #4** _____

Stuff needed:  a. _____

b. _____

c. _____

**Activity #5** _____

Stuff needed:  a. _____

b. _____

c. _____

Name: _____  Date: _____

## Chapter Two: *Planning Your Stay*

**Activity #6** _____

Stuff needed:  a. _____

b. _____

c. _____

**Activity #7** _____

Stuff needed:  a. _____

b. _____

c. _____

**Activity #8** _____

Stuff needed:  a. _____

b. _____

c. _____

Great work; you've thought of everything!

Oh, by the way, did I happen to mention that you will have NO electricity at your campsite? Did I mention that on this camping trip, it will rain for two whole days? Did I happen to mention that even though it is July, it cools off to 50 degrees at night? And—oh yes—did I mention that you can only bring with you what you can comfortably carry because you will need to park your car and walk at least one mile to your campsite? (Your tent materials will be provided by the park.)

Now that you know these little details, how will that change your plans? Will you change your activities, or will you change the stuff you plan to take?

_____

_____

_____

_____

_____

_____

_____

Name:_____ Date: _____

# Chapter Two: *Planning Your Stay*

All this brings us back to the importance of planning. Good planning lets us identify and solve problems before they happen so maybe they won't be problems after all. Good planning also lets us think all the way around an idea or trip or task so when something unexpected really does happen, we can make good decisions as quickly as we need to make them. Good planning lets us continually ask and practice answering the question, "What if ...?" So let's give it a try! Here is your first assignment:

Most of us have jobs or chores that we do around our homes. Take a few minutes to jot down the kinds of work that kids your age often do.

_____

_____

_____

_____

_____

Now, group the jobs that you listed above into two major categories.

| **Indoor jobs** | **Outdoor jobs** |
|---|---|
| _____ | _____ |
| _____ | _____ |
| _____ | _____ |
| _____ | _____ |

This time, group the indoor jobs and the outdoor jobs into two categories.

| **Indoor jobs I like to do** | **Outdoor jobs I like to do** |
|---|---|
| _____ | _____ |
| _____ | _____ |
| _____ | _____ |

| **Indoor jobs I don't like to do** | **Outdoor jobs I don't like to do** |
|---|---|
| _____ | _____ |
| _____ | _____ |
| _____ | _____ |

Name: _____ Date: _____

# Chapter Two: *Planning Your Stay*

Finally, we will put these categories into outline form. And this time, I will also ask you to give a reason why you like or don't like a job. (If you don't have four jobs in each category, leave that part of the outline blank.)

I. Jobs Kids Like Me Do Around the House (the title)

    A. Indoor jobs

        1. Indoor jobs I like to do (or at least don't mind doing)

            a. _____

                1. Reason: _____

            b. _____

                1. Reason: _____

            c. _____

                1. Reason: _____

            d. _____

                1. Reason: _____

        2. Indoor jobs I don't like to do

            a. _____

                1. Reason: _____

            b. _____

                1. Reason: _____

            c. _____

                1. Reason: _____

            d. _____

                1. Reason: _____

    B. Outdoor jobs

        1. Outdoor jobs I like to do (or at least don't mind doing)

            a. _____

                1. Reason: _____

            b. _____

                1. Reason: _____

            c. _____

                1. Reason: _____

            d. _____

                1. Reason: _____

Name:_____ Date: _____

# Chapter Two: *Planning Your Stay*

2. Outdoor jobs I don't like to do

a. _____

  1. Reason: _____

b. _____

  1. Reason: _____

c. _____

  1. Reason: _____

d. _____

  1. Reason: _____

This time, create a list of your favorite games. Think about all the kinds of games that you played when you were much younger, as well as the kinds of games you enjoy playing today. Take about five minutes and list as many games as you can. (You may need extra paper for your list!)

**My List**

1. _____  2. _____

3. _____  4. _____

5. _____  6. _____

7. _____  8. _____

Now try to put the games you listed into two major categories: Indoor Games and Outdoor Games. Look back at all the games you listed. Are there any groups (subcategories) of games within those major categories of indoor and outdoor games? Hint: Where are the games played: on a field, on a board, or on a screen? Do players play on teams, or do players play on their own against someone else? List your subcategories and the games that are examples of that subcategory. (You may need extra paper for this!)

A. Indoor games

  1. Subcategory: _____

    a. game: _____

    b. game: _____

  2. Subcategory: _____

    a. game: _____

    b. game: _____

B. Outdoor games

  1. Subcategory: _____

    a. game: _____

    b. game: _____

  2. Subcategory: _____

    a. game: _____

    b. game: _____

Name:_____ Date:_____

## Chapter Two: *Planning Your Stay*

A. Indoor games (continued)

  3. Subcategory: _____

    a. game: _____

    b. game: _____

B. Outdoor games (continued)

  3. Subcategory: _____

    a. game: _____

    b. game: _____

That is great! You are really becoming a *champion* at generating ideas and organizing them into an ordered outline!

Finally, let's suppose that your teacher has asked you to write a report on games. Take a *good look* at your outline of categories, subcategories, and examples of games. Is there anything else you might want or need to discuss about games to make your outline a map to follow as you write your report? **Correct!** Usually a report has some kind of *beginning* or *introduction* and ends with some type of *conclusion*—an ending statement that briefly reviews what you have said and ties everything together.

What are some things you could say in the introduction? Remember, an introduction helps the reader know what to expect and is interesting enough to make the reader want to keep reading. Try writing three to five sentences that might become your introduction to your report on games.

_____

_____

_____

_____

Share your introduction with at least three people who will share their introductions with you. Which do you like best and why? Now that you have heard some examples of intro-duction paragraphs—a group of sentences that work together to do a job, like introduc-ing—make any changes in your introduction that you think would make it better and re-write it.

_____

_____

_____

_____

Fabulous! Now guess what? Your teacher says that your re-port on games should have two major categories, you can only have three subcategories in each major category, and you can only talk about one example in each subcategory.

Name:_____ Date: _____

# Chapter Two: *Planning Your Stay*

Take a quick look back at your outline and decide: What subcategories will you pick, and which game example will you choose? Write your outline using the model provided.

### Title: Games

I.    Introduction to report on games

II.   Indoor games

    A. Subcategory: _____

       1._____

    B. Subcategory: _____

       1._____

    C. Subcategory: _____

       1._____

III.  Outdoor games

    A. Subcategory: _____

       1._____

    B. Subcategory: _____

       1._____

    C. Subcategory: _____

       1._____

IV.   Conclusion to report on games

You are really becoming organized! The last step is to estimate how many pages or partial pages you think you will use on each of the parts of your report. For example, you could probably use about half of one page on both the introduction and the conclusion. But the introduction and the conclusion should begin and end on "new" sheets to keep each separate from the rest of the report. About how much space do you think you would need for each of the examples in each of the subcategories? Would one-half of one page be too much or too little?

Write down your estimates, and then add up the number of the full and half pages to determine how long your paper might be. Then you will probably need to add one or two pages for the lists of resources you used. (We will be learning how to keep track of those resources in a later chapter. That list is called a "Works Cited" section.) So how long do you think your report on games could easily be? _____

The last part of the estimating involves thinking about how long it might take to find the information you will need, to take notes, and to recopy (either in your own handwriting or on the computer) for your final copy to hand in to your teacher. Be realistic! Be sure to give yourself enough time to do a good job.

Name: _____ Date: _____

## Chapter Three: *Packing Smart*

### Doing the Research

You have made your plan. You know where you want to end up, but now you need to know what to take. Researching is just like planning what you are going to take on your trip. In order to pack smart, you need to know more about it.

So you're going to write about Chicago. Where can you find information about Chicago? Brainstorm with the class about what resources will give you information about the city of Chicago. Make a list.

_____

_____

_____

_____

### Encyclopedias

When we pack smart, we need to start with a suitcase. A suitcase gives an overall coverage for the items we will need to take on our trip. One of the best resources to give an overall coverage of a topic is an encyclopedia.

Encyclopedias give general information on practically any topic. Some encyclopedias present even more specific information about one subject, such as science or history.

Encyclopedias are arranged alphabetically by topic. In order to pack smart, it is best to start with the **index volume** of the encyclopedia because it will give you the exact volume and page numbers for your topic, and it will save you a great deal of time. The index may also give you ideas or cross references for additional information on your topic.

The information in the encyclopedia on your topic is called an **article**. The authors of the article will appear at the end of the article. Sometimes an article will be "unsigned." This means that no author is listed. Often there will be a list of books, which is called a bibliography. A **bibliography** tells more about the topic. These titles may be found in the library and will help you "pack" or research for your "trip" or topic.

Go to the index volume of your encyclopedia and find the cross references for Chicago. List them here.

_____

_____

_____

_____

Name:_____ Date: _____

# Chapter Three: *Packing Smart*

Look at the bibliography at the end of the article in the encyclopedia. Pick the titles that fit in with your research plan and list them here.

_____

_____

_____

_____

_____

## Books

Now it's time to pack for your trip. This is where your plan becomes very useful. You don't want to take all of your clothes; you only want to take what you need. How do you know what you need? You look at your plan, and then decide you will only need summer-type clothing. Let's say you look at your research plan and find that you only want information on the history of Chicago, specifically Jane Addams. Where do you start?

A good place to start is the library. Books in school libraries and public libraries are arranged by the Dewey Decimal System. (However, it is not necessary to know the Dewey Decimal System to find a book in the library.) The library has a catalog that lists all the materials in the library by title, author, and subject. The catalog may be looked up either in a series of drawers or on a computer.

The card catalog is a series of drawers arranged alphabetically. The cards in the drawers list titles, authors, and subjects. The card gives the location of the book by identifying its Dewey Decimal number.

A Public Access Catalog, or PAC, is a card catalog on computer. To search a computer catalog, you will need to decide if you are going to search by the title of the book or article, author, or subject.

Let's pretend you have found a book that will help you learn more about Jane Addams. The book is called *Jane Addams: Crusader for the Poor* by Anne Shirley. To look up the specific book so you can locate it on the shelf, begin with the first letter of the title. In a card catalog you would look in the "J" drawer; in a PAC you would type in the title. You will see that the book has been given the Dewey Decimal number of B ADD S. To find this book, you may ask the librarian to help you.

Next, you want to find other books about Chicago. In the card catalog, you need to find the "C" drawer; on the PAC computer you request a "subject" search and type in "Chicago, Illinois". You will now see all of the books about Chicago. You will see a long list of titles. Do you need to check out all of these books? No, not every book about Chicago will give you the

Name: _____ Date: _____

# Chapter Three: *Packing Smart*

information you need. This is where you will use your plan. You can read the description of the book and decide which books you would like to look at.

Let's pretend you have the following list of books:

917.73 SMI Smith, Claire. *Architecture of Downtown Chicago*. Park Publishing, 1999.

328.773 JON Jones, Samuel D. *Chicago City Council Proceedings*. Everyman Press, 2000.

361.92 BUR Burger, Kathryn. *Hull House Revisited*. University of Campton Press, 1997.

B ADD WHI White, Randy. *Jane Addams: A Biography of Hope*. Larimer Publishing, 2001.

305.8 CAR Carter, Nancy. *Chicago Neighborhoods*. Circuit Court Press, 1992.

Which books on the list, by reading the title, would you use for your report on Chicago and Jane Addams? List four titles and their Dewey Decimal number or "call number" that you could use.

_____

_____

_____

_____

## Magazine Articles

You now have your suitcase and clothes for your trip. The encyclopedia gives the coverage of your topic, and books give you the items you will need in order to be more specific about your topic. Now, we need important items that perhaps aren't very big, but are still needed for a good trip. These items would be your toothbrush, toothpaste, shoes, socks, etc. Information from magazine articles are those small but necessary items that make your topic more current and interesting.

How do you find these articles? Again, your school or public library is the place to go. Think of the library as the grocery store of knowledge. It's not possible to personally own all of the magazines that are printed, but a library is able to subscribe to many different good quality magazines or journals.

Now that you are at the grocery store of knowledge, you must find out which magazine articles are about your topic. Just like going to the grocery store for toothpaste, you don't look in the vegetable aisle to find it. The library keeps all its magazines together and has special tools to find the articles you will need for your topic.

Name: _____    Date: _____

# Chapter Three: *Packing Smart*

Libraries have a resource called *The Reader's Guide to Periodical Literature*. This index has a listing of articles by topics. It gives the magazine title, article title, date, and issue for specific articles that are about specific subjects. There is an abbreviation code on the first page that identifies the magazines listed in the index.

Let's pretend that you want an article about Chicago. Go to the reference librarian and ask where *The Reader's Guide to Periodical Literature* is located. When you find it, you will notice that it is arranged alphabetically by topic. This means you need to look up "Chicago". If you want the most current information about Chicago, just as you would want a fresh tube of toothpaste for your trip, you start with the most recent index. Check the date!

When you go to the grocery store shelves to look for toothpaste, you will find many different brands. You will also find many different articles about Chicago. You will see entries that look like this:

New Evidence in the Historic Chicago Fire; s. dale
Chic His Jrnl 34:10-13 J '00

"New Evidence in the Historic Chicago Fire" is the title of the article. The article will be found in the magazine *Chicago History Journal*. The number 34 is the volume number of the magazine, and the numbers 10-13 are the page numbers of the article. J '00 is the issue January 2000.

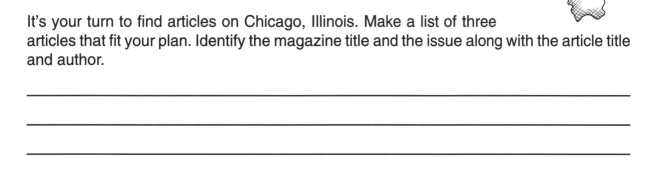

You may also find "see" and "see also" references that will lead you to more articles about Chicago that aren't listed directly under "Chicago." For example, you might see the following list:

Chicago, Illinois
See also
Windy City
Magnificent Mile
Gold Coast
See Illinois Cities

It's your turn to find articles on Chicago, Illinois. Make a list of three articles that fit your plan. Identify the magazine title and the issue along with the article title and author.

_____

_____

_____

_____

Many public libraries have a magazine index listed in their Online Public Access Catalog. You will find the magazine index listed under "Databases." Remember, you can always ask the librarian for help.

Name: _____     Date: _____

# Chapter Three: *Packing Smart*

A common magazine index that public libraries have is called *OCLC FirstSearch*. It gives you a listing of books, articles, documents, and so on. If you only want magazine articles, you can have the database search for only magazine articles by selecting that option. Just as you will want a new tube of toothpaste, you will want to organize your article search by the most recent article information.

If you were to search the "ArticleFirst" of *OCLC FirstSearch* for Chicago, Illinois, ranked by date, you might see a page that looks like the following:

23.   Latino Outreach: The Case of the Rudy Lozano Branch of the Chicago Public Library.
      Author: Hernandez, Hector R. Source: Illinois Libraries, 75, no. 5, (Fall 1993): 328-330
      Libraries: 1002

24.   Paths to Glory.
      Author: Kappe, Bale; Morse, Libby; Reynolds, Gretchen Source: Chicago, 42, no. 9,
      (September 1993): 58 Libraries: 556

25.   Rollin' on the River.
      Author: Reynolds, Gretchen Source: Chicago, 42, no. 6, (June 1993): 70 Libraries: 556

What does all of that mean? The title of the article is listed first and is underlined. For example: Rollin' on the River is the title of the article. It was written by Gretchen Reynolds. The article can be found in the magazine *Chicago*, issue 42, number 6, which was the June 1993 issue of *Chicago*. The article can be found on page 70. There are 556 libraries that have a copy of this magazine.

Do you need all of the tubes of toothpaste as well as several toothbrushes? No, and neither do you need all of the articles about Chicago! You will have to decide which articles you want to read; you can click on the title of the article, and it will give you a brief summary. This is like reading the label of the toothpaste. You might want a mint gel toothpaste instead of a peppermint paste. So you need to know what you are wanting to write about in order to choose which article you will need.

Now that you know which articles you want, how do you find them? Again, ask your librarian for help. If your library has the magazine you need, your librarian can show you where it is and help you check it out or find a place for you to read it in the library. However, the library may not have the magazine, so now what do you do? Your librarian can request the article from another library through Interlibrary Loan. (Think of your librarian as a tour guide through the store of knowledge.)

Name: _____  Date: _____

# Chapter Three: *Packing Smart*

### The Internet

As you continue packing, you might want to take along items such as a camera or a book. These items add to your comfort. Resources on the Internet can also add to your research. However, you must be careful that the information you find on the Internet is correct and not simply an advertisement.

You will use a search engine to look for information about your topic. It is very similar to using the Online Public Access Catalog in your library. Therefore, you will use the same process for looking up information on the Internet as you would in the computer library catalog.

One of the advantages of the Internet is that you can contact associations that provide you with current information about your topic. Remember that **.com** sites are commercial sites wanting to sell you something, and **.org** sites are organization sites that will provide information about the organization or association that sponsors that site.

If you have access to the Internet, use one of the search engines to look up information about Chicago, Illinois. You should access the website for the Chamber of Commerce of Chicago, Illinois. List four websites that would have information about Chicago, Illinois.

_____

_____

_____

_____

_____

_____

_____

You've now decided <u>what</u> you are going to pack. Now it's time to do the packing!

Name: _____ Date: _____

# Chapter Four: *Avoiding Lost Luggage*

## Citing Your Sources

Now you are ready to pack! In order to do this, you need to know what to pack and where you are going to pack your items. Also, if you want to avoid lost luggage, you will need to identify or label your luggage.

If you want to show where the information for your report comes from, you will have to cite your sources. The best way is to follow a "documentation style" to identify the source from which you are taking the information.

There are many different "documentation styles" to use. We will be using the Modern Language Association style, or "MLA."

Let's talk about taking notes. The easiest way is to use 3" x 5" index cards. You will use one card for each note or piece of information you find that is important to your topic. On each card, you should identify the source of the information. This is the citation information or the locator of your "luggage."

Your note card will look like this:
*Top Line:*
Citation Information

*Below Citation Information:*
Information from the resource. This information may be in the form of a direct quote or paraphrasing the information you have read.

You may use a direct quote, but you must give credit to the source of the information. This is where the correct citation information is used.

## Encyclopedias

Remember when we compared an encyclopedia to a suitcase for a trip? It provides the foundation for the rest of your research because an encyclopedia gives general coverage of the topic. So we need to identify the "luggage" where the topic begins.

Encyclopedias are considered reference books, so there is a certain style for the citation information. Remember that we talked about how articles in the encyclopedia can be signed or unsigned? There are two ways to cite the information based on whether the encyclopedia article is signed or not.

Name: _____     Date: _____

# Chapter Four: *Avoiding Lost Luggage*

Let's pretend that you are planning a report on Chicago, Illinois. You have a *World Book Encyclopedia* in your classroom, and you have found information on Chicago, but there is no author for the article. The citation is very simple; here is the information you will need.

1. Title of article
2. Title of encyclopedia
3. Year of publication

This information is easy to find. The title is at the beginning of the article—"Chicago, Illinois." The title of the encyclopedia can be found in several places. It is on the spine as well as on the title page of the book. In our case, the title of the encyclopedia is *World Book Encyclopedia*. The year of publication is found on the spine of the book. However, it can always be found on the title page of the book. In this case, we'll pretend the year of publication is 1999.

Now that you have all this information, what is the next step? You will write the information at the top of the note card in this way:

"Chicago, Illinois." <u>World Book Encyclopedia</u>. 1999 ed.

Simple, isn't it? But what if there is an author? You will simply need to identify the author, whose name is found at the end of the article in the encyclopedia. Let's pretend you are using the article on Jane Addams in the *World Book Encyclopedia*. At the end of the article, you might see the name Claire Jones. So, instead of beginning with the title of the article on your note card, you begin with the author's name. Your citation will look like this:

Jones, Claire. "Addams, Jane." <u>World Book Encyclopedia</u>.
     1999 ed.

Did you notice that when we went to the second line of the citation, it was indented? The second line and each line thereafter should be indented five spaces on the citation. It makes it easier to read. Also notice that there are two spaces after periods.

## Books

Now that you have identified your "suitcase," you must identify the items you will be taking with you on your trip. For your report, these items are the books you will be taking your notes from.

There are many ways to cite book resources according to the MLA style. The type of book determines how it is cited. The information you will need for the citation is whether there is one or more authors, no authors, if it is an anthology or collection, etc.

We will look at the basic form of citing a book resource. If you have a book that does not fit into one of the categories we will look at, you can talk with your teacher or librarian. They will help you find the information in the MLA Documentation Style Manual.

Name: _____ Date: _____

## Chapter Four: *Avoiding Lost Luggage*

Here is an example of a title page.

History
of the
Chicago Fire

First-Hand Accounts

By Samuel Smith

Quincy Publishing, Inc.
Quincy, IL

This is an example of a book by one author. You need the same information for this citation as you did for the encyclopedia. However, for this citation, we also must list the author, title, the city and state of the publishing company, the publishing company, and the date. Look at the title page example above. What information is missing? That's right, the date. When you turn to the next page, you will find the words "Copyright © 1986" near the top of that page.

Using this information, the citation for this book would look like this:
Smith, Samuel. <u>History of the Chicago Fire: First-Hand Accounts</u>. Quincy, IL: Quincy Publishing, Inc., 1986.

Now you try it! Here is a sample title page and second page. Write your own citation in the space below.

Jane Addams
and
Hull House

By Kathryn White

ABC Printers
New York, NY

Copyright © 1989
ABC Printers
New York, NY

_____

_____

_____

_____

_____

Name: _____ Date: _____

# Chapter Four: *Avoiding Lost Luggage*

If the book has two or three authors, you would list all of the authors' names in the order they appear on the title page. Here's an example:

Chicago's
Ethnic Cultures

By Nancy Carter,
Carolyn Seymour,
and
Jane Allan

Jumping Jacks Press
Chicago, IL

(on second page)

Copyright © 1991
Jumping Jacks Press
Chicago, IL

The citation should look like this:

> Carter, Nancy, Caroline Seymour, and Jane Allan. <u>Chicago's
> Ethnic Cultures</u>. Chicago, IL: Jumping Jacks Press, 1991.

If your book has more than three authors, you should list the first author only and refer to the remaining authors as *et al.* If there is no author listed on the title page, you will begin the citation with the title of the book and continue as before with the place of publication, the publisher, and the date.

## Articles

You have packed your clothes; now it's time to pack the other small essentials you will need for your "trip." For your report, this is the information you find in magazine or newspaper articles. This information will be more current than in books or encyclopedias.

The format for citing magazine and newspaper sources is very similar to that used for encyclopedias and books. Suppose you found a newspaper article about Hull House in Chicago. The article appeared in a paper called the *Chicago Daily Times*. (Note: This isn't a real newspaper.)

Name: _____    Date: _____

# Chapter Four: *Avoiding Lost Luggage*

Here is the information:

Article Title: Jane Addams' Hull House—A Chicago Landmark
Author: David Mark
Newspaper: Chicago Daily Times
Date: June 18, 2000
Page number: E10

Here is  the correct way the citation should be written:

Mark, David. "Jane Addams' Hull House—A Chicago Landmark."
    Chicago Daily Times  18 June 2000: E10.

Isn't this very similar to the citation for books? Just think of the newspaper as the publisher because that's what a newspaper does: it publishes articles. When you are writing out your note cards, this information would appear at the top of the note card, just as when you take notes from encyclopedias and books.

What if there is no author? You would begin with the title of the article and then give the rest of the information. It should look like this:

"Did Mrs. O'Leary's Cow Really Start the Chicago Fire?"
    Chicago Tribune  12 Jan 1991: 41.

Magazines are good resources for current information on a topic. They are compact but full of good information. How do you cite a magazine article? It's your turn to try. Here is the information:

Author: Alexander Shay
Title: The World's Fair in Chicago
Magazine: Chicago History Magazine
Date: March 18, 1998
Pages: 47–52

_____

_____

_____

_____

_____

Name: _____ Date: _____

# Chapter Four: *Avoiding Lost Luggage*

### Electronic Sources

You are on your way, but you're not finished packing! Today, many classrooms and people have encyclopedias on their computers, which are CD-ROM resources. The same basic information is required for a citation of this type of resource. Let's look at an example.

> "Chicago, Illinois." Encarta 1994. CD-ROM. Redmond, WA:
> Microsoft, 1993.

The one additional piece of information to include with an electronic resource is to list that it is in a *CD-ROM* format rather than the usual printed format.

### The Internet

Today we can research topics using the World Wide Web or the Internet. As researchers, you must be cautious about the information you find on the Internet. Some of the information is correct and very current, while other information is not very reliable. How do you tell the difference? Unfortunately, there is no way to tell whether the information given is correct. Generally, if you try sites that are associated with colleges and universities, accepted associations and organizations, and government organizations, the information is most likely dependable. It is always a good idea to discuss sites with your teacher or your librarian. How do you cite an Internet source? Just as in the other citation models, an Internet citation includes the same information in approximately the same order.

Suppose you find an Internet site about the Chicago Fire. It is the Chicago Historical Society's website. The article about the fire was written by John O'Leary with a title of "The Cow Who Started the Fire." The date of the website is October 12, 1999, and you found the article on February 14, 2001. The website address is http://chicagohissoc.org. The address of the article is http://chicagohissoc.org/ChicagoFire/history.sum.html. This is the information, listed in the order you will need it:

1. Author's name
2. Title of article
3. Date of electronic publication, posting, or the most recent update
4. Name of the sponsoring institution or organization
5. Date you accessed the material
6. Website address or URL (Universal Resource Locator) in angle brackets with a period at the end

This is what the citation should look like:

> O'Leary, John. "The Cow Who Started the Fire." 12 Oct. 1999.
> The Chicago Historical Society. 14 Feb. 2001
> <http://chicagohissoc.org/ChicagoFire/history.sum.html>.

Name: _____ Date: _____

# Chapter Four: *Avoiding Lost Luggage*

For a more detailed description of a citation for a website, consult the MLA Documentation Handbook.

Well, you're all packed. Now it's time to make a complete list of everything you've packed in your suitcase. For your report, you must make a list of all resources <u>used</u> to write your report. This means that if you had taken notes from a resource but these notes were not included in your report, then that resource will not be included on the "Works Cited" page. You only list the resources you used in your report.

There are some rules to follow when putting your "Works Cited" page together. The resources should not simply be listed in random order, but listed alphabetically by the first word of the citation. If you have correctly recorded the information on your note cards, this should be a simple task.

Here are all resources listed in this chapter. Try putting together a Works Cited page on the following page using the titles below.

"Chicago, Illinois." <u>World Book Encyclopedia</u>. 1999 ed.

Jones, Claire. "Addams, Jane." <u>World Book Encyclopedia</u>. 1999 ed.

Smith, Samuel. <u>History of the Chicago Fire: First-Hand Accounts</u>.
    Quincy, IL: Quincy Publishing, Inc., 1986.

Carter, Nancy, Caroline Seymour, and Jane Allan. <u>Chicago's</u>
    <u>Ethnic Cultures</u>. Chicago, IL: Jumping Jacks Press, 1991.

"Chicago, Illinois." <u>Encarta 1994</u>. CD-ROM. Redmond, WA:
    Microsoft, 1993.

Mark, David. "Jane Addams' Hull House—A Chicago Landmark."
    <u>Chicago Daily Times</u> 18 June 2000: E10.

"Did Mrs. O'Leary's Cow Really Start the Chicago Fire?"
    <u>Chicago Tribune</u> 12 Jan 1991: 41.

O'Leary, John. "The Cow Who Started the Fire." 12 Oct. 1999.
    The Chicago Historical Society. 14 Feb. 2001
    <http://chicagohissoc.org/ChicagoFire/history.sum.html>.

Since this is such an important part of a written report or term paper, we'll also discuss it in another chapter. So if you are not exactly sure how to do this, don't worry. And if you thought this was easy, you'll enjoy the review.

* Information on this chapter was taken from <u>Simon & Schuster Quick Access: Reference for Writers Second Edition</u> by Lynn Quitman Troyka, Prentice Hall, 1998.

Name: _____  Date: _____

# Chapter Four: *Avoiding Lost Luggage*

## Works Cited

_____

_____

_____

_____

_____

_____

_____

_____

_____

_____

_____

_____

_____

_____

_____

_____

_____

_____

_____

_____

Name: _____ Date: _____

## Chapter Five: *Bon Voyage!*

### Introductions and Conclusions

The words *bon voyage* mean "Have a good trip!" or "Have a wonderful voyage!" It is part of the trip before the trip actually begins. It has to do with thinking about and looking forward to the trip. So now you have a destination—the topic for your report or term paper. You have carefully packed for your travels—considered and chosen what resources and information will best fit your needs. And you have clearly marked your luggage so nothing will be lost—you have kept a very clear record of exactly where you found all of your information. That means that at last, you can begin to relax and think about the very real fun you will have as you actually start on your travels—your report.

*Did you say that I was going to have fun doing an assigned report?*

Yes, you heard me right! Work is only very *difficult* or *boring* if that is what you have decided it is. But if you think about doing a report or term paper as your chance to travel somewhere you have never been, to meet fascinating people who lived hundreds of years ago (or even right now), or to tell what you think really happened (or should happen), well, that makes everything seem a little different. (If you recall, there **were** some jobs you listed in a previous chapter that were jobs you really didn't mind doing, *right*?)

So we start at the beginning of your report—the **introduction**. The introduction of your report/term paper serves the same purpose as introducing a friend to anyone else.

By the way, just how would you introduce your best friend? Take a few minutes to think about it and jot down some things about your best friend that would convince your parents, grandparents, or even an aunt and uncle, that your friend would be a good person to invite along when you go to spend a week with them this summer.

_____

_____

_____

_____

_____

Let's look at what you wrote. Did you ...
1. Mention anything about *why* your best friend *is* your best friend?
2. Mention anything about how your friend looks, thinks, or acts?
3. Mention how much time you and your friend spend together and the things you do when you are together?
4. Mention that your friend would be NO TROUBLE AT ALL to have along on the visit?

Name: _____ Date: _____

# Chapter Five: *Bon Voyage!*

I'll bet your introduction tries to accomplish at least two things. I have a feeling you describe your friend and how well you get along, and then you try to convince your parents, grandparents, or your aunt and uncle, etc., that it would be a wonderful idea to let your friend come with you for the visit. (In other words, you state some important facts, and then you use those facts to convince someone to do something that you want done.)

Well, the introduction to your report/term paper would basically do the same thing. It would let your reader(s) know what the report/term paper is all about (the person, the place, the idea, the purpose of the report), and it would say it in a way that would make the reader want to keep reading. It cannot BE the report, but it gives just enough information about the report to make the reader want to turn the page and keep turning the pages to learn more.

*How long should an introduction be?*

The length of an introduction depends upon the length of the report/term paper. When we think about reports, we usually think about writing on one topic and not more than perhaps 3–5 pages. We should probably use paragraphs to discuss things about the topic, so an introduction for a report would probably need to be at least one paragraph.

A term paper is different from a report in that a term paper is usually much longer because it is more detailed. Instead of spending paragraphs talking about things, a term paper is often divided into chapters or sections. These chapters or sections have several pages and many paragraphs and discuss the details about the topic of that chapter. The introduction to a term paper would probably be at least a page because you would be saying some things about each chapter. Take a minute to look at some of your school books. Do they have an introduction? Where are they, and how long are they? Where is the introduction to this book, and how long is it? What kinds of things does this introduction do? What kind of information does it tell? (Did you read it before you began the book? And if you had, would it have made the rest of the book make more sense?)

The key to writing a good introduction is to know exactly what your report will say and how your report will be arranged to say it.

*How will I know exactly what will be in my report when I haven't written it yet?*

Some writers *think* their way through each part of their reports, having their ideas carefully planned and arranged on paper, just as you organized your ideas about the camping trip, the jobs that kids do, and games in Chapter Two. Then, all they have to do is look at their outlines, and they can write their introductions before they ever begin to write their reports.

Other writers claim that the best way to write an introduction is to write the whole report first. Then, if you change your written plans because you've found surprising information or change your mind about what you think, you won't need to completely rewrite your introduction.

　　　　　　　　33

Name: _____ Date: _____

# Chapter Five: *Bon Voyage!*

Which way do you think would be better, and why?

_____

_____

_____

_____

(Did you ever stop to think that when you see the coming attractions at the theater, those film clips are from movies that have been finished for months? The company that made the movie plans to show you just enough to make you want to come back and see the whole show ... Hmmm! Perhaps a good introduction is much like a good commercial!)

Anyway, let's get started writing great introductions—interesting word commercials that will sell your report or term paper.

*But HOW do I start? I can't just begin writing ... "This report is about _____ and I know you're going to think it's great!"*

Yes, you are right, that would be a ridiculous way to start. But there are a lot of really good ways to begin. Let's consider several and see what might work best for you.

Since I am one of those people who likes to write the introduction AFTER I've written most of my report, I like to think back about some unusual thing or things that I learned while doing my report. Then I can either include them in my introduction, or I might even turn my introduction into several riddles that can be answered only by reading the rest of my report. For example, I could say something like this.

He dreamed of attending West Point Military Academy, but he would fail the vision test. He failed as a farmer. He failed as an oil prospector. He failed as a businessman. Some say he would have failed as a politician if his friends hadn't worked hard for him. He had been vice president for less than ninety days when he got the news. President Franklin D. Roosevelt had died. Harry S Truman suddenly became the 33rd President of the United States and had before him the toughest decision of his life. Would he fail to make the right decision?

I could also begin by saying something like this.

Which president's eyes were so bad that as a teenager, he was not admitted to West Point Military Academy? Which president usually began each morning with a brisk walk outdoors around the White House? Which president decided that the White House was not a safe place to live when he watched his piano fall through the floor and halfway through the ceiling of the room below? And by the way, which president was in office when the United Nations was founded? The answer to all of these questions is the same: Harry S Truman, the 33rd President of the United States, and he is the subject of my report.

Name: _____ Date: _____

# Chapter Five: *Bon Voyage!*

Both of these introductions focus on facts I learned as I was doing my research. I found these details really amazing, and I thought most of my readers would be as interested as I was.

Now it's your turn. Think of someone you know a lot about or know really well. It could be a historical figure, or it could be a member of your own family. Try to think about interesting things that person has done or is doing. Think about what that person likes or dislikes. Think about where that person has been and what kinds of things he or she finds really interesting. (Perhaps this person can eat more pancakes than anyone else you know, or that person takes great pride in his or her garden or car.) Try writing an introduction for this person. First, try simply listing some facts about that person as I did in my first introduction of President Truman. Be sure to do this in pencil because you will probably need to stop and restart. That's okay; don't become discouraged.

_____

_____

_____

_____

_____

Fine! Now try turning things around and asking a few questions as I did. Ask questions that give hints about what a reader might find when reading the whole story about this person. Again, use a pencil.

_____

_____

_____

_____

_____

Which do you think would catch a reader's interest more? Share both of your introductions with someone else, and let that person decide which is better. (While that person reads your introduction, you should be sure to read his or hers, and don't forget to give your vote!)

Name: _____ Date: _____

# Chapter Five: *Bon Voyage!*

Now that you've tried introducing people, let's try introducing a report that you have written on either your school or your home. Remember, this is just an introduction, a short "word commercial" that would make a reader want to read your whole report to learn more. When you have finished, have at least two people read it and suggest how you might make your introduction better.

_____

_____

_____

_____

_____

Great work! So far, you've been focusing on introducing a topic by mentioning facts. However, there are other good ways to approach introductions to reports and term papers.

Suppose your report or term paper is about your state. Begin your introduction as if you and the reader(s) are in a small airplane and are about to land at an airport just outside the state capital. What kinds of buildings would you begin to see and recognize? What kinds of vegetation (trees, flowers, fields) would you begin to see as you approach? Would there be a lot of traffic, or would things be fairly quiet? Is there anything distinctive about the music you would hear inside the airport? Think about what makes your state capital typical of your state. As always, share your work with several others and ask for their suggestions.

_____

_____

_____

_____

_____

_____

Name: _____ Date: _____

## Chapter Five: *Bon Voyage!*

Pretend that your report or term paper is about some aspect of America's part in World War II. Also, pretend that you are living back then and are the same age that you are now. Describe where you are, what you are doing and wearing, and who you are with when one evening the radio program you are listening to is suddenly interrupted with the announcement that the United States is entering the war. What do you think about? What is the reaction of the people you are with? How do you think your life might change? Remember, this is an introduction to a report on America's part in World War II. It is not the whole report! Don't forget to have two or three people read and respond to your work. (Don't worry if you get stuck! Having someone else read your work is often the best way *to get just the idea* you need to become *unstuck*!)

_____

_____

_____

_____

_____

_____

_____

_____

Now you are supposed to choose some type of major purchase (a computer, a CD player, a new VCR, etc.), and you are to research and discuss reasons why one particular kind is the best to buy, based on your needs. Write an introduction to your report or term paper by briefly telling about the time that you or someone else bought the wrong kind and on one or two occasions things went really wrong. If the story is true, it is called an anecdote (**an**/eck/doat). If it is not true, it is just a good story. Either one can be a wonderful way to introduce your report!

_____

_____

_____

_____

_____

_____

Name: _____    Date: _____

# Chapter Five: *Bon Voyage!*

Here is the last exercise. You have just become my trusted assistant teacher. One of our students has given us this introduction to read, and we need to give back some suggestions on how to make it better. Your task is to read this and make as many improvements, including corrections, as you can suggest. When you find a mistake, underline it. I also asked the student to number each sentence, so if you think the sentences need to be moved around, you can simply list the corrected sentences in the order they should come. This student really needs your help! Thanks! (When you have finished, compare your corrections and suggestions to others in your class. Who in your class provided the most help to this student writer?)

(1) When my teacher said I had to rite a repart on one of the Presdints, I didn't know witch one to pick. (2) There have been so many of them. (3) Presdints like George Washigton and Abraham Lincon always go first, and I din't want my report to be jist like everybody else's repart. (4) I wanted to pick some obscewre fellow, somone I really didn't know much about. (5) Well, I began looking threw the list of men who have been Presdints, and you know what? (6) I discovered that I really didn't know much about vury mini of them! (7) I then decided that cents we had fourty-tree Presdints, I wood ask my best frend Pete to pick a nummer from one to fourty-tree. (8) didn't tell him why I needed for him to pick the number. (9) just tole him to pick a number. (10) Then I told him he couldn't pick nummer one or sixteen. (11) I didn't say those were the nummers for Washinton and Lincon. (12) So, Pete picked nummer twenty-seven. (13) The tweny-seventh Presdent of the United States jest hapened to be Mr. William H. Taft, and I shore didn't know nuthing about him! (14) When I told my teacher that I wunned William H. Taft, gess wat? (15) She asked me why I picked him. (16) Cents I wasn't shore how to explain my choice, I jest told her that it was a big serprise! (17) Well, the serprise was on me cause I had no idea what an ineresting fellow this Mr. William H. Taft really was.

Name: _____ Date: _____

# Chapter Five: *Bon Voyage!*

(18) I decided to arange my infermation into tree parts for this report. (19) first part will tawk about Mr. Taft's life before he become Presdint. (20) I will tell bout his famly and how his brothers and sisser would teese him and call him Big Lub because he was so big. (21) I will also talk bout how he went to school, became a lawer and juge, and how much he said he dint like polertics. (22) (His mother even said she shore woodn't want him to become Presdint!) (23) The secund part of my report will tell what happened in America and round the wurld while he was Presdint. (24) In fact, Mr. Taft had mini "fursts" as Presdint. (25) Some of his fursts involved basball, cheery trees, and gitting stuck in the white house. (26) (Mr. Taft was the bigest Presdent, standing sax feet tall and waying over 300 pounds. (27) In fact, one of the newspaper reparters said Mr. Taft looked like a bufalo—a big frendly one.)

(28) The last part of my report will tell why he did not win reelection as Presdint and what he did after he lost the lection. (29) Even then, Mr. Taft man-aged to dew sum things that no other Presdint has ever done—even to this day! (30) I think that maybe nummer twenny-seven might be my lucky nummer!

So what do you think? If you think any of the sentences need to be moved around, which ones would you switch?

_____

_____

_____

_____

_____

Name: _____ Date: _____

## Chapter Five: *Bon Voyage!*

The last thing that we need to mention is the conclusion portion of your report or term paper. It makes sense to discuss conclusions at the same time as introductions because a conclusion should briefly review what your report or term paper really **did** say. It should remind the reader of what your introduction said your report or term paper was going to discuss. But like the introduction, the conclusion is NOT the report all over again! It is a summary that simply mentions key points you want your reader to remember. **Because not all reports or term papers require a conclusion, be sure to ask your teacher if you will need to include one with your work.**

You just helped a student who wrote a 30-sentence introduction to a research paper on President William H. Taft. Your assignment is to take that introduction and turn it into a conclusion. You will need to rewrite it, remembering that the conclusion comes at the end of the report. You will also need to pick out only a few details you think are the most important for a reader to remember. And because a conclusion is supposed to be a brief summary, your conclusion must be no more than 12 sentences. Use the rest of this page for your writing, or you may want to use this page for your "sloppy copy," and use your own paper for the copy to show your teacher.

First, jot down what you think are the interesting or important details from the beginning, the middle, and the ending of the report on Taft that you think your reader should remember. Think through each sentence. (Is it really necessary to discuss every detail of how you chose Taft as the subject of your report?) Choose your words carefully!

_____

_____

_____

_____

_____

_____

_____

_____

_____

_____

_____

As always, trade your work with at least one other person for comments and suggestions before your teacher reads your conclusion.

Name: _____ Date: _____

# Chapter Six: *Are We Having Fun Yet?*

## Writing and Sharing What You've Learned

Now that you have completed the research and taken notes on your topic, you have organized your information into an outline, and you have thought about your introduction (which you may write either before or after the rest of the report) and your conclusion, you are ready to write the report itself. Great job! You can now focus on learning, enjoying, and writing to share all the fun.

So, you take out those notes and begin to write. Wait a minute! When you took the notes from the books, magazines, newspapers, or the Internet, did you copy word-for-word what was written down, or (after you read and thought about the information) did you put things into your own words?

If you copied information word-for-word from books, magazines, newspapers, or the Internet, you must treat that information differently because you are not just using general ideas that you found in every resource you used. You are using exact words that you found in probably only one source. That is called **quoting** your source. If you do this, you must name the author of the book, magazine article, etc., that you used. If you do not do this, you have just stolen someone else's writing, which is called **plagiarism**, and you can find yourself in some major trouble! Adult writers who have been found guilty of plagiarism have had to pay hundreds, and sometimes thousands, of dollars in fines and court costs. Some have lost their jobs, and all have lost the respect of readers and other writers. Students who plagiarize often find themselves getting either "F's" or "0's" on their assignments. Is this something you want to avoid? You bet!

Avoid plagiarizing by saying where you found these exact words. It isn't difficult, and there are several ways to do it. If your language arts book has a section called *Citing Your Sources*, use that plan. But before you begin to write, be sure to ask your teacher how he or she wants you to do this. This will make writing your report much easier.

No matter what system of citing your sources your teacher wants you to use, most of them will ask for the same kind of information. And it will save you SO MUCH TIME AND TROUBLE later if you do follow these steps as you use your notes and write your report!

To save time later, the first thing you will need to do is to keep a list of all the resources you use: books, magazines, newspapers, interviews, and Internet information. Eventually, you will use this list of books, etc., for the Works Cited page of your report. We will be talking about this much more in a later chapter.

Start keeping your list of books by first writing down the author's last name, then first name followed by a period. Then write the title of the book followed by a period; underline the title but NOT the period. Next, write the name of the city and the two-letter abbreviation for the state where the book was published followed by a colon. The last two things you will write will

Name: _____ Date: _____

# Chapter Six: *Are We Having Fun Yet?*

be the name of the company that published the book, followed by a comma, and the year the book was published, followed by a period. You have just made what is called a **book entry**. This is what it should look like. (Warning: These examples are pretend books, companies, etc., but the spaces and indentations are correct.)

> Dye, Rebecca. <u>The Last Book You'll Ever Need to Read on Wildlife</u>.
> Boston, MA: Whodunnit Press, 2000.

Now if there had been two authors for this book, this is the correct way to write it for the works cited page.

> Dye, Rebecca, and Carol Keller. <u>The Last Book You'll Ever Need to Read on Wildlife</u>.
> Boston, MA: Whodunnit Press, 2000.

*Hey, where do I find this information?*

It's usually found on the page following the title page. If it isn't there, it will be nearby.

*What do I write if I use an encyclopedia?*

Let's say you looked up *ferret* in the encyclopedia. You would write down the following information for your Works Cited page.

> Orth, Helen. "Ferret." <u>Truly Far-Out Encyclopedia of Wildlife and Weird
> Stuff</u>. 9th ed. 2000.

Notice that we still begin with the author of the article first. Then we write the name of the article in quotation marks with a period inside the quotation marks. This is followed by the name of the encyclopedia and the edition number, then the year it was published.

*What do I do if I use an article from a magazine?*

WHAT always goes first? Right! Write the name of the person who wrote the article (last name first), then the title of the article in quotation marks, the name of the magazine, the volume number, if listed, the year, and the page numbers. It will look like this.

> Keller, John. "Making My Own Fishing Tackle." <u>Indoor Crafts for Outdoor
> Fun</u> vol. 1 (1900): 55-60.

If you were going to put these on your Works Cited page, you would write each entry in alphabetical order by the author's last name. For example, you would list all the information I gave in this order: Dye, Keller, Orth.

Name: _____ Date: _____

# Chapter Six: *Are We Having Fun Yet?*

*So how does this help save time as I write? Why do I need to know this stuff?*

Good questions! If your teacher lets you use this system, then you begin writing your report as you would begin writing any assignment. If you find that you are going to use exact words or very specific thoughts from one of these sources, you must give them credit for the information, and you can easily do it as I did in the following example.

I think ferrets make remarkable pets because, in my opinion, they are truly amazing animals. According to Rebecca Dye, ferrets are the smartest creatures on the planet (51). In fact, they just might be the smartest animals in the universe (Orth, 4). They are even useful creatures as they shed unwanted and unnecessary fur. John Keller says, "Their shed hair makes championship-quality trout flies." (25) But as far as I am concerned, they just make fabulous pets.

You will notice that when I wrote something that Rebecca Dye thought and mentioned in her book, I put it in my own words, but I put the page number (51) to show the reader exactly where he or she could find out what the author actually said on page 51. In the next section, using information from Orth, I put my reference and page number at the end of the sentence, so the reader could easily look it up for himself/herself. In the last example, I used John Keller's *exact* words, so I put quotation marks around them and used the page number at the end of the quote.

I really like using this system, but again, you will need to ask your teacher how he or she wants you to do this. There are many very good systems that would be just as easy for you to use, so you really do need to know which system to use as you are writing your report. And now you know why.

So there you are, writing away and citing your sources, avoiding plagiarism, and having a great time describing all the things you are learning. It is **just** like being on vacation and sending postcards or letters to your friends, telling them about all the neat things you are seeing and doing.

However, letters and postcards that are full of spelling errors, have missing words, or have sentences that don't make any sense are not fun for anyone to read. If you want to have happy readers, you must be a writer who is easy to read as well as being a writer who has something interesting to say.

Name: _____     Date: _____

# Chapter Six: *Are We Having Fun Yet?*

Let's take a look at some writing that made some readers very unhappy! What are some of the problems with the following portions of student reports? If you find a word that is not spelled correctly, circle it and correct it. If you find a word needing a capital letter or a missing piece of punctuation, use proofreading marks and fix it. If you think the sentences are not in the correct order, number them in the order you think they should come. The examples are double-spaced to make it easier for you to make corrections.

**Example #1**

The dictinary states that an iguana is "... any of various large, herbivorous, typically dark-colored, tropical American lizards ..." But when i think of an iguana, i think of my pet  Ziggy In my rport, I will tell you all abut these speshal cretures by telling you all about Ziggy. first, I will tell you where iguanas like Ziggy live naturly then i will discus what they need to stay alive like food and shelter. Finally, I discuss take care of Ziggy and the kind of care he gets whin he goes to the vetrinarian.

_____

_____

_____

_____

_____

_____

_____

_____

_____

_____

_____

Name:_____ Date:_____

## Chapter Six: *Are We Having Fun Yet?*

**Example #2**

      The costline of mexico stretches nearly 1,800 miles along the golf of mexico and

the caribbean sea, and almost 4,500 miles along the pacific ocean and the golf of california

Mexico owns several small islands along both coasts. however according to L. Smith,

most of these are uninhabited. the eastern coast of Mexico has amost no bays. Excellant

bays along the western cost serve as habors for three port cities, the most famous of

which is Acapulco. The warm, sunny climate, beautiful clean white beaches, and the

outstanding recraational fishing in waters off the west coast. Attract thousands of visitors

evry year

_____

_____

_____

_____

_____

_____

_____

_____

_____

_____

_____

_____

Name: _____ Date: _____

# Chapter Six: *Are We Having Fun Yet?*

**Example #3**

The Channel Islands are geographicaly clos to france, lying as little as eight miles off the continent's coastline. But as far as histry goes, these islands (jersey, guernsey, alderney, sark, herm, jethou, and a few other tiny islets) have been basically british for more than a thousand years. They were part of normandy when william the Conqueror invaded englind in 1066 and became its king, and they remained part of britain when normandy was reunited with the rest of france

This heritage has given the Channel Islands a curiously mixed identity. Partly self-governing, and with a hodgepodge of english and french laws, they have french as their ofishall language, yet almost everyone who lives on the islands speeks english these people ishoe therer own bank notes (paper mony), coins, and postege stamps, yet british curency is accepted without any questin the food is french, but there habits and manners are english.

The Channel Islands attract over two millun tourists every yeer the Islands' popu-larity is partly dew to the feeling both british and french visiters have of being in another country. The Islands are also very popular because of there usually good weather also, the Islands are popular because no two of them is exactly the same for example jersey the biggest and most southern of the islands is the most lively turist center with a wide choice of hotles resterants and other kinds of entertainment. jersey got its name from Norman soldiers who called it gersey—they're word for a grassy island. The island's capitol is St. Helier. About half the people who live on jersey live in St. Helier. St. Helier has a great beech called St. Aubin's Bay nearby is Elizabeth Castle, built in the 1500s

Name: _____ Date: _____

# Chapter Six: *Are We Having Fun Yet?*

and named after queen elizabeth I by sir walter raleigh who was a governor of Jersey during World War II Jersey was occupied by german troops in fact, visitors can take tours of the bunkers to see how the German troops lived and worked there jersey also has one of europe's most interesting zoos, serving as home to several rare and endangered speshes.

Guernsey is the other main island. In years past, the island it made most of its money from agreculture but in the last few years it has turned to tourism and banking (finance) for most of its employment. the capitol city is St. Peter Port which is dominated by the town's only church many vacationers in Guernsey like to visit cassel cornet, a mideval fortress that protected the governor during a rebellion in 1651.

On the smaller islands such as Alderney, Sark, and Herm, there is little to do except eat sleep hike and enjoy beautiful rocky beaches and cliffs. Alderney has a small golf course Sark, the smallest state in europe, is ruled by a man called the Seigneur who has the authority to act like a feudal lord. It is a position that is inherited, so someday, one of his children will become the Seigneur. He has outlawed automobiles divorce adoption income tux and owning pigeons (the reason he is the only one who can own a pigeon is that once, there were too many pigeons on the island and they were eating too much of the grain meant for cattle so the Seigneur decided he would be the only one who could keep the birds) because the Seigneur has outlawed cars, people who live there as well as tourists travel around the tiny island by bicycle, horse-drawn carriage, or on foot Herm is only about 1 1/2 miles long and 1/2 mile wide. This tiny island is actually the private property of one man who farms part of the land and leases out some of it to

Name: _____ Date: _____

# Chapter Six: *Are We Having Fun Yet?*

people to run one very small hotel a restaurant and a few shops most tourists who go to

Herm only go there for its peace and quiet and to visit Shell Beach, a stretch of shoreline

that, instead of being sand, is made of milluns of tiny seashells that begin their journey in

the golf of mexico and are washed all the way up to europe by the golf streem the last

island, Jethou, is owned by one family tourists are not welcome.

_____

_____

_____

_____

_____

_____

_____

_____

_____

_____

_____

_____

_____

_____

_____

_____

Name: _____     Date: _____

# Chapter Seven: *Souvenirs and Snapshots*

## The Appendix and Works Cited Portion of Your Work

*The appendix!!? An appendix is something that people have. Mine made me so sick last summer that the doctor took it out! Want to see the scar?*

Uh, no thanks ... I'm sorry you were sick, and I'm glad you are feeling better now. I guess you didn't know that humans are not the only things having something called an appendix. Some kinds of apes and even rodents also have them. A report or term paper can also have an appendix. Regardless of where you find it, any appendix does basically the same thing.

In animals, an appendix is a narrow tubelike sac that is part of the large intestine. Medical specialists think that hundreds and hundreds of years ago, the human appendix helped us digest the many raw fruits and vegetables we ate. Over time, we have begun to eat more cooked and processed foods, and specialists believe that the appendix has become useless as far as digestion goes. But it is still there, and the appendix can become infected when what we have eaten passes through the intestines and, for some reason, becomes trapped in it. Bacteria begins to grow (oh, yuck!), causing the appendix to become more swollen and infected until it can make a person dangerously ill.

Like that little saclike pouch in your intestines, the **appendix** in a report or term paper is the spot where you put things that don't exactly fit anywhere else. For example, instead of putting a map in your first chapter, where you mention the location of a city, you tell your reader to see Exhibit One, a map, in the appendix. (Usually each item you put in your report's appendix is called an exhibit, and each exhibit is numbered. If the first exhibit is a map, you would want to label it E#1: Map (which means exhibit number one is a map).

What other things could you put in the appendix of a report or a term paper? Well, it depends on your topic. Sometimes students put pictures of important people in the report. Charts, letters, graphs, drawings, or anything else that would be important to help your reader better understand your report could be placed in the appendix.

But remember, when my appendix becomes too full or has something that really shouldn't be there, what happens? That's right! It becomes irritated, infected, and often needs to be removed. The same thing can happen to your report's appendix. If it becomes swollen with too much information or the wrong kind of information, it can make the rest of your healthy report look *sick*. Carefully choose what to include in your term paper's appendix.

Name: _____     Date: _____

# Chapter Seven: *Souvenirs and Snapshots*

Think about the kinds of things you might use as exhibits to place in your report's appendix if your report were about *you*. Try to think of at least ten items. Be specific!

1. _____   2. _____

3. _____   4. _____

5. _____   6. _____

7. _____   8. _____

9. _____   10. _____

Great ideas! Now let's think about that report on games we outlined earlier. Can you generate a list of six kinds of items having to do with games you could include in your report's appendix?

1. _____   2. _____

3. _____   4. _____

5. _____   6. _____

Great! Now you are ready to complete the very last pages of your report or term paper: **Works Cited**. This is the part of your paper where you list all the books, magazines, encyclopedia articles, and online sources you used to complete your report or paper. In the last chapter, I mentioned that knowing which system for doing your research and writing before you do either could save you a lot of time. There are several different ways to write and cite (give credit for information). No one way is any better than the other. Just be sure to ask your teacher which system you should use.

I often use the system developed by the Modern Language Association, or MLA. Using this system means that I don't have to write an extra page for something called endnotes. It also means you will not have to include something called footnotes, which are put at the bottom of

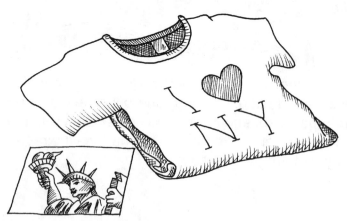

the page. I simply mention the author in a sentence, and then I put the page number of the information I took from the source in parentheses ( ). The examples of sources I used in Chapter Six follow the MLA guidelines. Each piece of information given about a book, magazine article, entry in an encyclopedia, or online (Internet) resource is put in a certain order to allow the reader to find out exactly where my information can be found.

50

Name: _____     Date: _____

# Chapter Seven: *Souvenirs and Snapshots*

Here are examples of the ways different resources would be written on the Works Cited page in a report or term paper. (Again, these are not real resources! They are created to show you how to write real resources in your report or term paper.)

*... a book with an author*

Dye, Rebecca.  <u>The Last Book You'll Ever Need to Read on Wildlife</u>.
　　Boston, MA:  Whodunnit Press, 2000.

*... a book with two authors*

Dye, Rebecca, and Carol Keller.  <u>The Last Book You'll Ever Need to Read on Wildlife</u>.
　　Boston, MA: Whodunnit Press, 2000.

*... an entry in an encyclopedia or a dictionary*

Orth, Helen.  "Ferret."  <u>Truly Far-Out Encyclopedia of Wildlife and Weird
　　Stuff</u>.  9th ed.  2000.

*... an article in a magazine or periodical*

Keller, John.  "Making My Own Fishing Tackle."  <u>Indoor Crafts for Outdoor
　　Fun</u>  vol. 1 (1900):  55-60.

*... online information*

Online information is handled just like information in regular print except you must add the date you accessed the information and the complete network address. Here are some examples. Put as much information as you can find in the order used in the examples. If you cannot find all of the information, cite as much as you can.

*... a project or information database*

　　<u>Dytannic Online</u>.  Vers. 53. 2.28.  Feb. 2001.  Encyclopedia Dytannic.
　　　　28 Feb. 2001  <http://www.ed.com/>.

　　<u>The Fairytale Channel Online</u>.  2001.  Fairytale Channel.  28 February 2001
　　　　<http://fairytalechannel.com/>.

　　<u>Twentieth Century Ferret Stories</u>.  Ed. Helen Orth.  2000.  Wildlife Dept.,
　　　　University of Nowhere.  20 Dec. 2000  <http://www.wd.un.edu>.

Name: _____ Date: _____

# Chapter Seven: *Souvenirs and Snapshots*

*... an article in a newspaper*

> Wackey, Ima. "No One Likes Spaghetti More Than I Do." <u>Weird Times on
> the Web</u>. 16 June 2000  25 June 2000  <give the complete network address>.

\* Note: On this one, you will see that there are two dates listed. The first date, 16 June 2000, is the date the article was first published. The second date, 25 June 2000, is the date you accessed the article.

*... an article in a magazine*

> Wackey, Youra. "My Sister Loves Spaghetti." <u>Food Unglued</u>. 17 June
> 2000.  26 June 2000  <give the complete network address>.

That covers most of the types of resources you will be using. Remember that some resources are better than others. If you are not sure that you have chosen a good resource or the best one available, ask your teacher or librarian.

Now you are ready to practice writing a Works Cited page, the last page of any report or term paper. Do you have any questions before we start?

*Yes! Suppose I found a book or an article or something with ed. following it. Who is this ed guy? What do I do?*

You found a book that an editor has put together using work from several others. The following example is how such a book would look on your Works Cited page.

*What if I use two books from the same author?*

It would look like this.

Dye, Rebecca, ed.  <u>The Last Book You'll Ever Need to Read on Wildlife</u>.
　　Boston, MA:  Whodunnit Press, 2000.

---,  <u>The Next to Last Book You'll Ever Need to Read on Wildlife</u>.
　　Boston, MA:  Whodunnit Press, 1999.

Name: _____  Date: _____

# Chapter Seven: *Souvenirs and Snapshots*

*Suppose I found a resource without an author mentioned. What do I do?*

In that case, put the second required piece of information as the first. Keep the information in the required order.

*Okay! You said I should put everything in alphabetical order when I list my resources on the Works Cited page. Let's say I don't have any author for The Last Book You'll Ever Need to Read on Wildlife. Do I alphabetize that as a "T" for The or an "L" for Last?*

You would use the *"L"* for <u>Last</u>. Many titles begin with *the, a,* or *an*. We would NOT use those words to alphabetize.

*Here is my last question! I see you have put some spaces between lines. Why?*

If you are handwriting your report, you should ask your teacher if you need to skip lines, etc. If you are going to complete your report or term paper on a computer, you need to plan on double-spacing everything. (That means you will skip lines throughout your entire report or term paper—even on the Works Cited page.)

For word processing your report or term paper, you should use standard white, unlined paper, 8 1/2 inches wide x 11 inches long. The first line of your report or term paper will be one inch from the top of the page, and the last line should be one inch from the bottom of the page. You should plan to leave a one-inch margin on both the left and right sides of the page. Put page numbers in the upper right-hand corner, one-half inch from the top of the page, and one inch from the right edge of the page. Instead of saying page 2, page 3, and so on, you can replace the word *page* with your last name. For example, my second page would read *Dye 2*. In this way, the reader will know that this paper belongs to you.

When putting entries on your Works Cited page, begin each at the left margin. Indent the lines needed for the rest of that entry, as you would for starting a new paragraph. Periods (.) are followed by two spaces unless it is part of an abbreviation. Periods after an abbreviation are followed by only one space. Question marks (?), exclamation points (!), and end quotes (") are followed by two spaces. All other punctuation marks are followed by one space.

Name: _____ Date: _____

# Chapter Seven: *Souvenirs and Snapshots*

Well, trusty assistant teacher, here is the Works Cited page from a student who is in serious need of your help! Circle any errors. If the entries are out of order, number them in the order they should come. To save space, I did not skip lines; you will not need to correct that.

Works Cited

C. r. Brumback. "Vacationing for mental health." <u>Graduate</u> 1 (2001): 6.

<u>Camping trips in the Wilderness</u>. Natchez, MS: Nobody, inc., 1985.

Robert Dye. <u>Your vacation dollar</u>. Chicago, IL: perma press, 1965

broker, jacob. "i'd rather stay with grandma." toybox 6 (1999): 5–10.

Dye, Rebecca. <u>The Last book you'll ever need to read on wildlife</u>. Boston, MA: Whodunnit Press, 2000.

P. Germann <u>Museums of the midwest</u>. chicago, IL: wood press, 1988.

Will Green. <u>The right formula for family trips</u>. N.Y., NY: villa, inc. 2000.

Therlee Fedup. "Traveling without Reservations." <u>Hotel</u> 2 (1999): 1.

P. Germann. "Postcards, souvenir spoons, and tokens: souvenirs from vacations past." <u>memorabilia</u> 52 (1986): 12.

Pat Gore. "Expecting Company: When Family comes to Visit." Grandparent 3(2001): 1.

Emma Green. "Packing light? Don't forget your boots!" <u>Vacation travel tips</u> 37 (1998) 128–132.

Lefty Hand. <u>Medical Supplies for vacation emergencies</u>. New York, NY: nineoneone Press, 1975.

Will Green. "When Nature calls: camping with baby." <u>modern traveler</u> 11 (2000):27.

<u>Hysterical channel online</u>. 1999. Hysterical channel. 1 April 1999 <http://hystericalchannel.com/>.

Name: _____  Date: _____

# Chapter Seven: *Souvenirs and Snapshots*

Jarret Keller.  <u>Vacation Photography</u>.  Chicago, IL: JennJan, Inc.: 2001.

M. mcManus.  <u>Midwestern golf getaways</u>.  Dallas, TX: Parsenta Press, 1997.

john  keller.  "Making my own fishing tackle."  <u>Indoor Crafts for Outdoor
    Fun</u>  vol. 1 (1900): 55–60

M. McManus.  <u>Southwestern golf getaways</u>.  Dallas, TX: Parsenta Press, 1998.

Pete Moss.  "Was that really poison ivy?" <u>Edible plants illustrated</u>
    9 (2000): 9.

Kurt Keller.  <u>Guide to camping in America's national parks</u>.  Decatur, IL:
    Carol Press, 1982.

Helen Orth.  "Snakes."  <u>Truly far-out encyclopedia of wildlike and weird
    stuff</u>.  9th ed. 2000.

Curly Noodle.  "Quick meals for campouts."  <u>Digestion</u>  3(1999): 4.

Ali Veatch.  "Are We There, Yet?" Games to play on Bus Trips."  <u>Cruiser</u>
    19 (1995): 27–40.

Heather Timm.  "Don't forget the sunscreen."  <u>Beaches</u>  6 (2001): 25.

Barney Pryor.  "Traveling with your pet."  <u>Modern Veterinarian</u>
    10 (2000):  11–13.

Marcus Veatch.  <u>traveling with younger siblings: a survival guide</u>.
    Springfield, IL:  roadwarrior Press, 2000.

Helen Orth.  <u>Preparing Balanced Meals in Your RV: A Moving
    Experience</u>.  Stoplight press, 1994.

Barney Pryor.  "Good Dog: The obedient pet goes camping."
    <u>Illinois Traveler</u>  4 (2001): 1.

Chad Timm.  "Best Buys, Early Flights."  <u>Beaches</u>  6 (2001): 16.

K. Zoonhite.  "Allergy Country: When Hay Fever Hits."  <u>Modern
    Backpacker</u>  4 (2001): 1.

Name: _____ Date: _____

# Chapter Eight: *Home Movies*

## Sharing Your Work With an Audience

Now that you are back home and unpacked from that big trip, you are probably looking forward to telling and showing your friends all about where you went and what you did. If you took pictures, you sent them to be developed so you could relive all the fun you had. You probably have even written something about the pictures on the back of each one to remind yourself of some details. If you like to do scrapbooks, you have probably already set things up to show what you did each day.

Getting your report or term paper ready for an audience (your teacher or your classmates) requires the same thought and preparation as putting your vacation pictures and souvenirs in some kind of order. If either presentation is to be a success, you must have things in the right order; you must make sure everything is neat; and you must have things positioned to look interesting.

Let's give your report or term paper one quick check to be sure about proper order.

Your report or term paper should be in this order:

_____ Title page (title of report, your name, and the date the report is submitted)

_____ Introductory page or paragraph describing what the report is about

_____ Body of the report

        _____ I followed my teacher's requirements about paper.

        _____ I followed my teacher's requirements on margins.

        _____ All sentences are really sentences.

        _____ Each sentence begins with a capital letter and ends with a period, a question mark, or an exclamation point.

        _____ Words are correctly spelled.

        _____ Paragraphs have topic sentences and are either indented or are in block form as my teacher requested.

        _____ Paragraphs are in the right order, making the details in my report make sense.

        _____ The report does what it is supposed to do. It does not stray from my assigned topic. If it is supposed to answer a question, it answers it.

        _____ If I used exact words from a magazine, book, or online source, I put quotation marks around those words and gave the source of those words to avoid plagiarizing.

        _____ My report is the length my teacher requires.

Name: _____ Date: _____

# Chapter Eight: *Home Movies*

_____ Conclusion, if required by teacher

_____ Appendix, if necessary

     _____ All entries are neat.

     _____ There are no errors in spelling or punctuation.

     _____ All entries are in the order mentioned in my report, are neatly and correctly labeled, and are numbered in order.

     _____ All entries are directly related to my report so it will make sense to my audience.

_____ Works Cited

     _____ I have listed the books, magazines, articles, and online resources I used or found most helpful in writing my report.

     _____ I put my sources in alphabetical order by the author's last name. (If I couldn't find the author's name, I continued with the information I did have in the correct order.)

     _____ I carefully followed the examples to make sure I used all the necessary information in each entry in my Works Cited.

_____ Front and back cover, if required by teacher

Now that your report is ready for reading, let's think about any other items you might want to include.

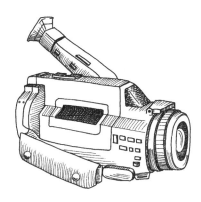

Most of us like to take pictures while we are on our trips. They help us remember exactly what the place or event was like and our enjoyment while we were there. Pictures, slides, and videos are wonderful ways to share an experience that is difficult to put into words. For example, pictures and slides can show specific examples of the people, places, and events you are describing. Videos can help show steps in a process, can help recreate events and/or situations, and can show things changing as they are happening.

If you are going to use pictures or slides, you will need to be sure that they are very clear and are large enough to show what you want to be seen. If you are going to be passing pictures around for people to see, you may want to put those pictures in an album or in plastic sleeves to protect them. If you are going to use pictures in books, you may want to make a copy of the

Name: _____ Date: _____

## Chapter Eight: *Home Movies*

picture to pass around. If you are going to use a book, be sure to put a marker in the pages you want your audience to see.

If you are using special equipment, be sure you know how to properly operate it. Check for good focus, lighting, and sound. It is always a good idea to use a new video cassette as you begin your taping. That way, you can be sure you are not recording over something else that is important, or you can avoid having your audience see something you don't want them to see before or after the presentation. *(How embarrassing!)*

If you are to make an oral presentation (a short speech) about your report, you may want to use your written introduction as a starting place. Practice reading your introduction out loud until you almost know it by heart. If you do this, you will feel so confident when it is your turn to speak that you can relax and tell, not read, your introduction or speech.

Whatever you do, remember that you have worked hard and have actually enjoyed learning about your topic, so enjoy sharing what you have learned with others in your class. Emphasize what you learned and found the most interesting. If someone asks a question that you don't know, be honest and say that you don't know, but that you will try to find out. Good reports will always lead to more questions, which lead to even more good reports. So while you are patting yourself on the back with one hand, jot down those unanswered questions with the other hand. Who knows? Those questions that need to be answered just might take you on your best "trip" yet! Bon voyage and happy landing!

# Answer Keys

**Chapter 4: Citing Your Sources (p. 26)**

Book Citation:
White, Kathryn. <u>Jane Addams and Hull House</u>.  New York, NY: ABC Printers, 1989.

**Chapter 4: Citing Your Sources (p. 28)**
Magazine Article Citation:
Shay, Alexander. "The World's Fair in Chicago." <u>Chicago History Magazine</u>  18 March 1998: 47-52.

**Chapter 4: Citing Your Sources (p. 30–31)**

Carter, Nancy, Caroline Seymour, and Jane Allan.  <u>Chicago's Ethnic Cultures</u>.  Chicago, IL: Jumping
    Jacks Press, 1991.

"Chicago, Illinois." <u>Encarta 1994</u>.  CD-ROM.  Redmond, WA: Microsoft, 1993.

"Chicago, Illinois." <u>World Book Encyclopedia</u>. 1999 ed.

"Did Mrs. O'Leary's Cow Really Start the Chicago Fire?" <u>Chicago Tribune</u>  12 Jan. 1991:  41.

Jones, Claire.  "Addams, Jane." <u>World Book Encyclopedia</u>. 1999 ed.

Mark, David.  "Jane Addams' Hull House—A Chicago Landmark." <u>Chicago Daily Times</u>  18 June 2000:  E10.

O'Leary, John.  "The Cow Who Started the Fire."  12 Oct. 1999.  The Chicago Historical Society.
    14 Feb. 2001.  <http:// chicagohissoc.org/ChicagoFire/history.sum.html>.

Smith, Samuel. <u>History of the Chicago Fire: First-Hand  Accounts</u>.  Quincy, IL:  Quincy Publishing, Inc., 1986.

**Chapter 5: Bon Voyage! (p. 38–39)**

    (1) When my teacher said I had to <u>rite</u> a <u>repart</u> on one of the <u>Presdints</u>, I didn't know <u>witch</u> one to pick. (2) There have been so many of them. (3) <u>Presdints</u> like George <u>Washigton</u> and Abraham <u>Lincon</u> always go first, and I <u>din't</u> want my report to be <u>jist</u> like everybody else's <u>repart</u>. (4) I wanted to pick some <u>obscewre</u> fellow, <u>somone</u> I really didn't know much about. (5) Well, I began looking <u>threw</u> the list of men who have been <u>Presdints</u>, and you know what? (6) I discovered that I really didn't know much about <u>vury</u> <u>mini</u> of them! (7) I then decided that <u>cents</u> we had <u>fourty-tree</u> <u>Presdints</u>, I <u>wood</u> ask my best <u>frend</u> Pete to pick a <u>nummer</u> from one to <u>fourty-tree</u>. (8) __ didn't tell him why I needed for him to pick the number. (9) _ just <u>tole</u> him to pick a number. (10) Then I told him he couldn't pick <u>nummer</u> one or sixteen. (11) I didn't say those were the <u>nummers</u> for <u>Washinton</u> and <u>Lincon</u>. (12) So, Pete picked <u>nummer</u> <u>tweny</u>-seven. (13) The <u>tweny</u>-seventh <u>Present</u> of the United States <u>jest</u> <u>hapened</u> to be Mr. William H. Taft, and I <u>shore</u> didn't know <u>nuthing</u> about him! (14) When I told my teacher that I <u>wunned</u> William H. Taft, <u>gess</u> <u>wat</u>? (15) She asked me why I picked him. (16) <u>Cents</u> I wasn't <u>shore</u> how to explain my choice, I <u>jest</u> told her that it was a big <u>serprise</u>! (17) Well, the <u>serprise</u> was on me <u>cause</u> I had no idea what an <u>ineresting</u> fellow this Mr. William H. Taft really was.

    (18) I decided to <u>arange</u> my <u>infermation</u> into <u>tree</u> parts for this report. (19) ___ first part will <u>tawk</u> about Mr. Taft's life before he <u>become</u> <u>Presdint</u>. (20) I will tell <u>bout</u> his <u>famly</u> and how his brothers and <u>sisser</u> would <u>teese</u> him and call him Big Lub because he was so big. (21) I will also talk <u>bout</u> how he went to school, became a <u>lawer</u> and <u>juge</u>, and how much he said he <u>dint</u> like <u>polertics</u>. (22) (His mother even said she <u>shore</u> <u>woodn't</u> want him to become <u>Presdint</u>!) (23) The <u>secund</u> part of my report will tell what happened in America and <u>round</u> the <u>wurld</u> while he was <u>Presdint</u>. (24) In fact, Mr. Taft had <u>mini</u> "<u>fursts</u>" as <u>Presdint</u>. (25) Some of his <u>fursts</u> involved <u>basball</u>, <u>cheery</u> trees, and <u>gitting</u> stuck in the <u>white house</u>. (26) (Mr. Taft was the <u>bigest</u> <u>Presdint</u>, <u>standing</u> <u>sax</u> feet tall and <u>waying</u> over 300 pounds. (27) In fact, one of the newspaper <u>reparters</u> said Mr. Taft looked like a <u>bufalo</u>—a big <u>frendly</u> one.<u>)</u>

    (28) The last part of my report will tell why he did not win reelection as <u>Presdint</u> and what he did after he lost the <u>lection</u>. (29) Even then, Mr. Taft managed to <u>dew</u> <u>sum</u> things that no other <u>Presdint</u> has ever done—even to this day! (30) I think that maybe <u>nummer</u> <u>twenny</u>-seven might be my lucky <u>nummer</u>!

# Answer Keys

**Chapter 6: Are We Having Fun Yet? (p. 44)**
Example #1

> *dictionary*
> The (dictinary) states that an iguana is "... any of various large, herbivorous, typi-
>
>                                                          I                          I
> cally dark-colored, tropical American lizards ..." But when i think of an iguana, i think of
>
>          ⊙   *report*              *about*    *special*   *creatures*
> my pet Ziggy. In my (rport) I will tell you all (abut) these (spesha) (cretures) by telling you all
>
>          F                                                   *naturally* ⊙T  I   *discuss*
> about Ziggy. first, I will tell you where iguanas like Ziggy live (naturly) then i will (discus)
>
>                                                                    *how to*
> what they need to stay alive, like food and shelter. Finally, I discuss, take care of Ziggy
>
>                            *when*                   *veterinarian*
> and the kind of care he gets (whin) he goes to the (vetrinarian)

**Chapter 6: Are We Having Fun Yet? (p. 45)**
Example #2

>      *Coastline*    M                                    *Gulf*  M
> The (costline) of mexico stretches nearly 1,800 miles along the (golf) of mexico and
>
>       C          S                              P        O        *Gulf*  C
> the caribbean sea, and almost 4,500 miles along the pacific ocean and the (golf) of california⊙
>
>                                                           H
> Mexico owns several small islands along both coasts. however, according to L. Smith,
>
>                                      T                    *almost*        *Excellent*
> most of these are uninhabited. the eastern coast of Mexico has (amost) no bays. (Excellant)
>
>        *coast*          *harbors*
> bays along the western (cost) serve as (habors) for three port cities, the most famous of
>
> which is Acapulco. The warm, sunny climate, beautiful, clean, white beaches, and the
>
>        *recreational*
> outstanding (recraational) fishing in waters off the west coast, Attract thousands of visitors
>
> *every*
> (evry) year⊙

# Answer Keys

## Chapter 6: Are We Having Fun Yet? (p. 46–48)
Example #3

*geographically close*

The Channel Islands are ~~geographicaly~~ ~~clos~~ to france, lying as little as eight miles

*history*

off the continent's coastline. But as far as ~~histry~~ goes, these islands (jersey, guernsey,

*England*

alderney, sark, herm, jethou, and a few other tiny islets) have been basically british for

more than a thousand years. They were part of normandy when william the Conqueror

invaded ~~engind~~ in 1066 and became its king, and they remained part of britain when

normandy was reunited with the rest of france.

This heritage has given the Channel Islands a curiously mixed identity. Partly

*official*

self-governing, and with a hodgepodge of english and french laws, they have french as

*issue their* *money* *postage*

their ~~ofishall~~ language, yet almost everyone who lives on the islands ~~speeks~~ english.

*currency* *question* *their*

these people ~~ishoe~~ ~~there~~ own bank notes (paper ~~money~~), coins, and ~~postege~~ stamps, yet

british ~~curency~~ is accepted without any ~~questin~~ the food is french, but ~~there~~ habits and

manners are english.

*million* *year*

The Channel Islands attract over two ~~millun~~ tourists every ~~yeer~~ the Islands' popu-

*due* *visitors*

larity is partly ~~dew~~ to the feeling both british and french ~~visiters~~ have of being in another

*their* *and*

country. The Islands are also very popular because of ~~there~~ usually good weather ~~also,~~

~~the Islands are popular~~ because no two of them is exactly the same for example jersey,

*tourist*

the biggest and most southern of the islands is the most lively ~~turist~~ center with a wide

*hotels restaurants* *their*

choice of ~~hoties~~ ~~resterants~~ and other kinds of entertainment. jersey got its name from

Norman soldiers who called it jersey—they're word for a grassy island. The island's

*capital*

~~capitol~~ is St. Helier. About half the people who live on jersey live in St. Helier. St. Helier

*beach*

has a great ~~beech~~ called St. Aubin's Bay nearby is Elizabeth Castle, built in the 1500s

and named after queen elizabeth I by sir walter raleigh, who was a governor of Jersey.

during World War II Jersey was occupied by german troops in fact, visitors can take

tours of the bunkers to see how the German troops lived and worked there jersey also

has one of europe's most interesting zoos, serving as home to several rare and endan-

*species*

gered ~~speshes.~~

*agriculture*

Guernsey is the other main island. In years past, the island made most of its

*capital*

money from ~~agreculture~~ but in the last few years, it has turned to tourism and banking

(finance) for most of its employment. the ~~capitol~~ city is St. Peter Port which is dominated

*Castle C*

by the town's only church many vacationers in Guernsey like to visit ~~cassel~~ cornet, a

*medieval*

~~mideval~~ fortress that protected the governor during a rebellion in 1651.

On the smaller islands such as Alderney, Sark, and Herm, there is little to do

except eat sleep hike and enjoy beautiful rocky beaches and cliffs. Alderney has a small

golf course Sark, the smallest state in europe, is ruled by a man called the Seigneur who

has the authority to act like a feudal lord. It is a position that is inherited, so someday,

one of his children will become the Seigneur. He has outlawed automobiles, divorce,

*tax*

adoption, income ~~tux~~ and owning pigeons the reason he is the only one who can own a

pigeon is that once, there were too many pigeons on the island and they were eating too

much of the grain meant for cattle so the Seigneur decided he would be the only one

who could keep the birds because the Seigneur has outlawed cars, people who live

there as well as tourists travel around the tiny island by bicycle, horse-drawn carriage, or

on foot Herm is only about 1 1/2 miles long and 1/2 mile wide. This tiny island is actually

the private property of one man who farms part of the land and leases out some of it to

people to run one very small hotel a restaurant and a few shops most tourists who go to

*It is*

Herm only go there for its peace and quiet and to visit Shell Beach a stretch of shoreline

*millions*

that, instead of being sand, is made of ~~millune~~ of tiny seashells that begin their journey in

*Gulf* *Gulf Stream*

the ~~golf~~ of mexico and are washed all the way up to europe by the ~~golf~~ ~~streem~~ the last

*and*

island, Jethou, is owned by one family tourists are not welcome.

# Answer Keys

**Chapter 7: Works Cited (p. 54-55)**

WORKS CITED

Brumback, C. R.   "Vacationing for Mental Health."  <u>Graduate</u>  1 (2001): 6.

Broker, Jacob.  "I'd Rather Stay With Grandma."  <u>Toybox</u>  6 (1999): 5–10.

<u>Camping Trips in the Wilderness</u>.  Natchez, MS: Nobody, Inc., 1985.

Dye, Rebecca.  <u>The Last Book You'll Ever Need to Read on Wildlife</u>.  Boston, MA: Whodunnit Press, 2000.

Dye, Robert.  <u>Your Vacation Dollar</u>.  Chicago, IL: Perma Press, 1965.

Fedup, Therlee.  "Traveling Without Reservations."  <u>Hotel</u>  2 (1999): 1.

Germann, P.   <u>Museums of the Midwest</u>. Chicago, IL:  Wood Press, 1988.

---.  "Postcards, Souvenir Spoons, and Tokens: Souvenirs from Vacations Past."  <u>Memorabilia</u>  52 (1986): 12.

Gore, Pat.  "Expecting Company: When Family Comes to Visit."  <u>Grandparent</u>  3  ( 2001): 1.

Green, Emma.  "Packing Light? Don't Forget Your Boots!"  <u>Vacation Travel Tips</u>  37 (1998)  128–132.

Green, Will.  <u>The Right Formula for Family Trips</u>.  New York, NY: Villa, Inc., 2000.

---.  "When Nature Calls: Camping with Baby."  <u>Modern Traveler</u>  11 (2000): 27.

Hand, Lefty.  <u>Medical Supplies for Vacation Emergencies</u>.  New York, NY: Nineoneone Press, 1975.

<u>Hysterical Channel Online</u>.  1999.  Hysterical channel.  1 April 1999.  <http://hystericalchannel.com/>.

Keller, Jarret.  <u>Vacation Photography</u>.  Chicago, IL: JennJan, Inc.: 2001.

Keller, John.  "Making My Own Fishing Tackle."  <u>Indoor Crafts for Outdoor Fun</u>  Vol. 1  (1900): 55–60.

Keller, Kurt.  <u>Guide to Camping in America's National Parks</u>.  Decatur, IL: Carol Press, 1982.

McManus, M.  <u>Midwestern Golf Getaways</u>.  Dallas, TX: Parsenta Press, 1997.

---.  <u>Southwestern Golf Getaways</u>.  Dallas, TX: Parsenta Press, 1998.

Moss, Pete.  "Was That Really Poison Ivy?"  <u>Edible Plants Illustrated</u>  9 (2000):  9.

Noodle, Curly.  "Quick Meals for Campouts."  <u>Digestion</u>  3 (1999): 4.

Orth, Helen.  <u>Preparing Balanced Meals in Your RV: A Moving Experience</u>.  Stoplight Press, 1994.

---.  "Snakes."   <u>Truly Far-Out Encyclopedia of Wildlife and Weird Stuff</u>.  9th ed. 2000.

Pryor, Barney.  "Good Dog: The Obedient Pet Goes Camping."  <u>Illinois Traveler</u>  4 (2001): 1.

---.  "Traveling With Your Pet."  <u>Modern Veterinarian</u>  10 (2000): 11–13.

Timm, Chad.  "Best Buys, Early Flights."  <u>Beaches</u>.  6 (2001): 16.

Timm, Heather.  "Don't Forget the Sunscreen."  <u>Beaches</u>  6 (2001): 25.

Veatch, Ali.  "Are We There, Yet? Games to Play on Bus Trips."  <u>Cruiser</u>  19 (1995): 27–40.

Veatch, Marcus.  <u>Traveling With Younger Siblings: A Survival Guide</u>. Springfield, IL: Roadwarrior Press, 2000.

Zoonhite, K.  "Allergy Country: When Hay Fever Hits."  <u>Modern Backpacker</u>  4  (2001): 1.